MELODY • LYRICS • CHORDS

W9-AUF-648

HENDRIX

SMASH HITS

THE COMPLETE LYRICS AND LEAD SHEETS FOR FOURTEEN SONGS
from the digitally remastered, re-release of the Reprise album,
Smash Hits by the Jimi Hendrix Experience

INCLUDES DETAILED NOTES AND COLOR PHOTOGRAPHS FOR EACH COMPOSITION

Introductory and historical notes by Noë Goldwasser
Discographical research by Michael Fairchild
Photo research by Bill Nitopi

Photographs by Chuck Boyd/Flower Children Ltd.

Art Director • Richard Slater
Editorial Director • Noë "the G" Goldwasser

Released under the supervision of Alan Douglas for Bella Godiva Music, Inc.

Exclusively distributed by

Hal Leonard Publishing Corporation

7777 West Bluemound Road
P.O. Box 13819 Milwaukee, WI 53213

CONTENTS

A HENDRIX PRIMER

Smash Hits was one of the five Jimi Hendrix lp's released while Jimi was alive. There were *Are You Experienced?*, *Axis: Bold as Love*, and *Electric Ladyland* — all on Track in England and Reprise in the US. And then there was *Band of Gypsys*, recorded live at the Fillmore East, New York, on New Year's Eve, 1970, a "contractual obligation" record done for Capitol to fulfill the terms of a lawsuit. *Smash Hits* and *Experienced?* have the common dubious distinction of being the only Hendrix lp's on which the US label saw fit to change the song selection. Hendrix was an lp artist to American fans, whereas English fans, who knew him first, knew him from the singles that began to be released in the UK as early as December, 1966 ("Hey Joe"/"Stone Free"). The Reprise people saw fit to remove "Red House," "Can You See Me?" and "Remember" from the US version, replacing them with songs that were hit singles to English fans: ""Purple Haze," "Hey, Joe," and "The Wind Cries Mary."

The English version of *Smash Hits*, released by Track in April, 1968, was more of a "hits" compilation, consisting as it did of songs which had made it to the higher reaches of the English charts. In England, some of these songs had not appeared on the *Experienced?* lp, but were known to the fans as singles. The track list for *Smash Hits* in England went like this: "Purple Haze," "The Wind Cries Mary," "Can You See Me?" "51st Anniversary," "Hey, Joe," "Stone Free," "The Stars That Played With Laughing Sam's Dice," "Manic Depression," "Highway Chile," "The Burning of the Midnight Lamp," and "Foxey Lady."

The Reprise version was released almost a year later, and remained on the *Billboard* charts for 17 weeks, reaching its highest position on that chart, #6, on August 8, 1969. It was on the Top Ten chart during the week of the Woodstock Festival. These statistics were compiled by my discographical collaborator on this tome, historian Michael Fairchild, who also notes ironically that "an interesting aspect of the *Smash Hits* album is that none of the songs were 'Smash Hits' in the US. The highest position reached here by any of the singles was #20 for 'All Along the Watchtower' (*Billboard*, September 28, 1968, on the charts for eight weeks). In the UK, 'Hey Joe' reached #4, 'Purple Haze' reached #3, and 'The Wind Cries Mary' reached #6." Some of the other cuts were apparently designated "smash" because they

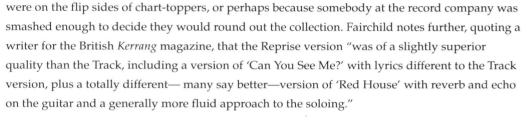

were on the flip sides of chart-toppers, or perhaps because somebody at the record company was smashed enough to decide they would round out the collection. Fairchild notes further, quoting a writer for the British *Kerrang* magazine, that the Reprise version "was of a slightly superior quality than the Track, including a version of 'Can You See Me?' with lyrics different to the Track version, plus a totally different— many say better—version of 'Red House' with reverb and echo on the guitar and a generally more fluid approach to the soloing."

The US version gave fans and collectors four tunes they wouldn't otherwise have on US releases: a studio "Red House," "Stone Free," "Can You See Me?" and "Remember." However, it did not have "51st Anniversary," "Laughing Sam's Dice," "Highway Chile," and "Midnight Lamp." The track list of the US version goes like this: "Purple Haze," "Fire," "The Wind Cries Mary," "Can You See Me?" "Hey Joe," "All Along the Watchtower," "Stone Free," "Crosstown Traffic," "Manic Depression," "Remember," "Red House," and "Foxey Lady." Some cassette versions of *Smash Hits* have sides one and two reversed.

Recently, Hendrix Estate producer Alan Douglas, in conjunction with Reprise, has put out a new version of the *Smash Hits* compilation, using the best masters from the US version and adding two songs from the UK one, "51st Anniversary" and "Highway Chile." The cuts on this new collection have been remastered and treated with all the kid-glove care that the wonders of modern digital recording can afford them. As such, the newest version of *Smash Hits* constitutes a new addition to the Hendrix oeuvre, a revisionist tribute to the more rousing efforts of a true genius of the guitar. The collection is one of movers and shakers, numbers that astonished listeners the first time they were heard. As a collection, it hovers in the realm of the physical more than the metaphysical—except for the otherwordly rendition of Dylan's "All Along the Watchtower," which can be seen as both rousing and transcendent.

The songs are not—like those on *Axis* and *Ladyland*—experimental or totally *out* surrealistic tone poems of sound, or studio-obsessed manipulations of tape and technology. But there is plenty of guitar double-tracking, phasing, fuzz, and flange, tricks which were used by Hendrix and his engineers to heighten the musical impact in a way that had never been done before the initial release of these recordings. They rock with thunder today as they did then. That's why they will always be classics of modern music. Listen to them with the respect that is their due—you are in the presence of greatness.

—Noë "the G" Goldwasser
Hendrix Library Editor

© N. Carter

PURPLE HAZE

Jimi was in his dressing room at London's Upper Cut Club having a brainflash inspiration of whimsy when he wrote a long poem on a notepad. It was early 1967, and Jimi was being called the "wild man of pop" by the English press. The Upper Cut date was one of a series of club gigs wherein Jimi was blowing the minds of the English pop aristocracy.

He described the story behind the song to a Swedish journalist: "Well, it's about this guy, this girl turned this cat on, you know [*laughs*], and he doesn't know which way he's going, you know, he doesn't know what's happening, really. He doesn't know if it's, you know, tomorrow or just the end of time for instance, you know?"

It was the first example of Jimi's use of Roger Mayer's effects boxes. "Purple Haze," "Fire," and "The Wind Cries Mary" were recorded at Olympic Studios during the week of February 3, 1967, two weeks after Jimi met Roger and Roger had shown him his Octavias and fuzzboxes that would transform Jimi's guitar sound irrevocably. "All the boxes I made for Jimi were called Octavia," said Roger later, "but they were each optimized for different specific sounds. One that was used on 'Purple Haze,' for instance, gives you an octave above [what you play]. But it's more than that...like putting something between two mirrors...it's doubled but it's more than doubled, because the doubling goes way out." The fuzz-drenched song was released March 18, 1967, and entered the English charts at #39 a week later. It charted as high as #4.

Purple Haze

By Jimi Hendrix

FIRE

This was among the initial flurry of songs that Jimi worked out with Eddie Kramer at Olympic Studios for the first album, *Are You Experienced?* but it was in live performance that the song truly showed its spark, literally. The Experience had a very important gig at Finsbury Park on March 31, 1967, opening for such teenybopper-approved acts as The Walker Brothers, Cat Stevens, and Englebert Humperdinck. Up until then, Jimi's wild antics were typified by a lot of jumping around onstage and tricks like playing the guitar with his teeth. For "Fire," the set-closer whose lyrics implored an imaginary young girl to let Jimi get warmed by her sexual heat, it was suggested by journalist Keith Altham and heartily endorsed by manager Chas Chandler that Jimi jazz up the act by actually lighting the guitar on fire.

At the end of the song, where Jimi says, "I have only one itching desire/ Let me stand next to your fire," Jimi went into action. As David Henderson described it in his important biography, *'Scuse Me While I Kiss the Sky,* "Jimi soloed on the upbeat tag-out that stretched on until he got the lighter fluid out. He almost blew it. Jimi went down on his back to pour the lighter fluid over the guitar. Lighting the matches seemed to take forever. Finally he got a light. Rolling over and hovering over his guitar he applied the match to the lighter fluid and immediately flames leaped, twelve feet high. He rocked back on his haunches and then over on his back, clutching his hands. People on both sides of the stage went berserk. To many in the audience it seemed as if Jimi Hendrix had self-immolated his body, like the Buddhists were doing in Vietnam—burning themselves in public. There was awe, freaky terror, and delight in the crowd as Jimi bounded up and disappeared backstage. The ovation was shattering. They howled in shock."

Fire

By Jimi Hendrix

Intro

Al– right!___ Now dig this, ba—by! You don't

1st Verse

care for me, I don't–a care a–bout__ that, you got a new fool,__ ha! I

like it like __ that. I have on – ly one–a burn–in' de–sire, _____

Chorus

let me stand __ next to your fire! ___ Hey! Let me stand __ next to your

Let me stand __ next to your fire! Whoa,__ let me stand,
fire!__ Let me stand __ next to your fire! ___

_____ ba – by! Let me stand. _____ Yeah,__ ba – by!
Let me stand __ next to your fire! Let me stand __ next to your fire! ___

Lis–ten here, ba–by, an' stop act–in' so cra–zy. You say your

I have on – ly one–a itch–in' de–sire,__ (spoken) let me stand_next to your fire! _____

Chorus
D(add9)   C(add9)   D(add9)   C(add9)

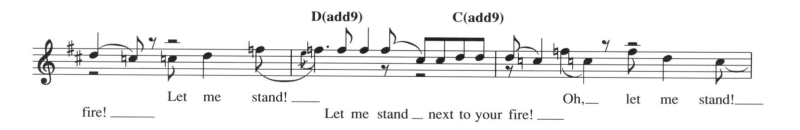

(Mss sta!)   Yeah! _____   let me   stand, __   ba – by!
Let me   stand __ next to your   fire! _____   Let me   stand_ next to your

D(add9)   C(add9)

Let   me   stand! ____   Oh,__   let   me   stand!____
fire! _____   Let me stand __ next to your fire! ____

D(add)   C(add9)   **Bridge**
D

—   Ow!   Ah, __ move o – ver,_
Let   me _____ stand next to your fire!_____

C(add9)   A

__ Rov–er,__   and let   Jim–i take o–ver!   Yeah, you know what I'm

talk(in') a – bout!　　　　Yeah!__　　　Get on with it ba – by!

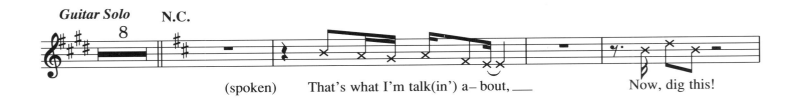

Guitar Solo N.C.

(spoken)　That's what I'm talk(in') a– bout, ___　　Now, dig this!

(D)

Ha!　　　　　Now lis–ten, ba–by!　　　You try to

3rd Verse
N.C.(D)

give me your mon–ey,　you bet–ter save it, babe,　　save it for __ your ___

rain – y　day.__　　I have on – ly one-a burn–in' de–sire,__　　let me stand __ next to your

Chorus
D(add9)　　　　　　　　　　C(add9)

fire, _____ ha!　　　　Ow!　　　Uh, let me stand!
　Let me　stand __ next to your fire!____

THE WIND CRIES MARY

"The Wind Cries Mary" was released in May, 1967 as a single, and went as high as #6 on the *Melody Maker* chart on June 3, 1967. Interestingly, that was a day after the release of the Beatles' *Sgt. Pepper*, which went straight to the top of the *MM* chart. The next week, Jimi went to the States and played Monterey. So that was the vibe at the time of this song's release. *Sgt. Pepper*, peace and love. With its very Dylanesque lyrics—"A broom is drearily sweeping up the broken pieces of yesterday's life. Somewhere a queen is weeping. Somewhere a king has no wife"—"Wind" was totally appropriate at the time.

Mitch Mitchell told *Guitar World* in 1985: "Keep in mind that a lot of the stuff was composed in the studio, or Jimi had a rough idea, or Jimi had a demo. For instance, 'The Wind Cries Mary' was cut on a Wednesday in Kingsway Studios, it was done as a demo. We had two goes at it, it was rough and ragged, so we went back and did it on Friday, and it was technically more proficient but it didn't have the feeling."

Chas Chandler told *International Musician* in 1980: "The tape operator at Olympic at that time was George Chkiantz...he was really into thinking up new sounds. Roger Mayer and George would sit huddled up thinking up ideas about sounds and how you could misuse the equipment....When we did 'The Wind Cries Mary,' Jimi had the idea for the song the night before, when we were in to do 'Purple Haze.' I think we were recording at the end of the day, and we found we had about 20 minutes left....I said, 'Just make a demo of it for the next time we come in.' We ended up recording that song in those 20 minutes, and there's five overdubbed guitars on that—and he'd never even played the song before!"

The Wind Cries Mary

Words and Music by Jimi Hendrix

CAN YOU SEE ME?

This song appears on the English (Track) version of *Are You Experienced?* but not the American (Reprise) one. The song was never released as a single, but it was a staple of Hendrix' early club dates, where he would take the opportunity of an elaborate solo in the middle bridge section. A version of it was recorded at a concert at the Flamingo Club in London on February 4, 1967, says Hendrix historian Michael Fairchild. The r&b boogie shuffle structure of the song lent itself to that kind of improvisation, and it shared that structure with songs by other sixties psychedelic-era groups like Cream and some other shuffles by Hendrix. The same riff turns up in Jimi's version of "Rock Me Baby." This is not to say that Jimi plagiarized himself, but rather, like all true artists, he established a signature for that type of song and kept returning to it for the rest of his career. In the world of art, the comparison holds up well when you analyze the work of Pablo Picasso. Certain ways of approaching a line or a curve or a color can be seen throughout his very prolific career. In the world of rock guitar, Clapton comes to mind. Clapton will always get from point A to point B in a chord change via the same step-like series of notes. It's his signature, developed when he first began to learn the blues.

There was a blistering version of "Can You See Me?" at the Monterey Pop Festival. You can hear it on *Jimi Plays Monterey,* the soundtrack recently culled from the Alan Douglas/D.A. Pennebaker-produced *Hendrix at Monterey* film. Unfortunately, you won't be able to see Jimi play the tune on the film or video version of that production, since the cameramen did not catch it. Douglas and Pennebaker wound up using it in the film with a sequence of an artist painting a Hendrix mural as the visual. It is used to open the film, rather than in the order it was played at Monterey.

Can You See Me?

By Jimi Hendrix

HEY JOE

"**H**ey Joe" dates back to Hendrix' pre-England days in Greenwich Village, when he was soaking up Dylan and the blues and playing in pass-the-hat clubs like the Cafe Wha? It was developed by Tim Rose from a folk song in the "Frankie and Johnny" mold, but the recording he made of it went nowhere...except into the repertoire of local Village groups and that of one James Marshall Hendrix. Jimi told *Melody Maker* in 1967: "'Hey Joe' is a traditional song and it's about 100 years old. Lots of people have done different arrangements of it, and Tim Rose was the first to do it slowly. I like it played slowly. There are probably thousands of versions of it fast by the Byrds, Standelles, Love, and others." The Leaves, a Los Angeles band, had a local hit with it in 1966.

When Chas Chandler took Jimi to England, "Hey Joe" was the first song they recorded, and the first single released by the new Jimi Hendrix Experience on December 16, 1966. They'd recorded a version of the song that they were not satisfied with. They then took it to the newly installed young engineer at Olympic Studios, Eddie Kramer, who invested it with the kind of studio wizardry that the team of Kramer and Hendrix were to become famous for in years to come—elaborate overdubbing, deepening of the bass and drum sounds, and a totally inventive use of feedback and distortion.

Chandler paid for the sessions out of his own pocket, and took the single to Decca, where it was turned down. Track finally released it, to their credit. "Hey Joe" entered the English charts on January 11, 1967, at #48. By February 4, it made it to #4 in *Melody Maker*. Legend has it that the song was the most-requested number on any of Hendrix' gigs, and it's box-office status was to haunt the later Hendrix, intent on delivering more poetic, surrealistic, and spacy sounds to the masses.

Hey Joe

Words and Music by Billy Roberts

ALL ALONG THE WATCHTOWER

imi put a lot of obvious love and mystery into his rendition of this Dylan song. "I felt like 'Watchtower' was something I had written but could never get together," he told *NME* in March, 1969. "I often feel like that about Dylan. Every time I perform his 'Like a Rolling Stone' it makes me feel so good—as though I had taken something off my mind....The singles are for the little kids."

Dylan felt the same way about Hendrix' appreciation. He wrote in the liner notes to his 1985 *Biograph* collection: "I liked Jimi's record of this and ever since he died I've been doing it that way. Funny, though, his way of doing it and my way weren't that dissimilar. I mean, the meaning of the song doesn't change like when some artists do other artists' songs. Strange, though, how when I sing it I always feel like it's a tribute to him in some kind of way....The last time I saw him was a couple of months before he died. He was in that band with Buddy Miles. It was an eerie scene. He was slouched down in the back of a limousine. I was riding by on a bicycle. I remember saying something about that song, 'The Wind Cries Mary,' it was a long way from playing behind John Hammond. That was my favorite song of his—that and 'Dolly Dagger'....I don't know, it was strange, both of us were a little lost for words. He'd gone through like a fireball without knowing it. I'd done the same thing, like being shot out of a cannon....I was thinking about him the other night—I really miss him a lot, him and Lennon....'All Along the Watchtower,' it probably came to me during a thunder and lightning storm. I'm sure it did."

The song was released as a single in England, on Track, October 18,1968. The English single was backed with "Long Hot Summer Night." The US version, with "Burning of the Midnight Lamp," reached #20 on the US chart, and charted on Billboard for eight weeks. It was, of course, included on Jimi's masterpiece, *Electric Ladyland*.

All Along The Watchtower

Words and Music by Bob Dylan

STONE FREE

his song was released as the flip side of Jimi's first single, "Hey Joe," on December 16, 1966, also the air date of The Experience's first tv show, an appearance on the seminal British rock 'n' roll show, *Ready, Steady, Go* with The Troggs (who did "Wild Thing"), The Merceys, and future Yardbird Keith Relf. The band viewed the broadcast on a tv set in manager Chas Chandler's apartment, before their gig at Chistlehurst Caves, actual caves in Kent where rock concerts were held at the time, which happened to be where Jimi first sat down to chat with electronic wizard Roger Mayer. It was there that Roger brought his experimental Octavias and other electronic effects boxes that Jimi used later (more on this in the introduction to "Purple Haze," above).

The intro has the psychedelic whammied-out raga sound of weirded-out Hendrix, but immediately after comes the cowbell-paced r&b riff that many of Jimi's early compositions were built on. Just as Jimi alternates between two chords a whole step apart in the riff, he also alternates between the classic r&b sound and the cosmic shuffle. This is Jimi's essence: clambering from his blues and r&b roots into the stratosphere, taking the music *out*, where he can be, as the chorus sings, "Stone free! To ride the breeze. Stone free! To do what I please." The chorus shows that, at the very beginning of his songwriting process, Jimi was using the central metaphor from his parachuting days—the notion of flight as freedom, or "riding the breeze."

Stone Free

By Jimi Hendrix

CROSSTOWN TRAFFIC

"Tire tracks all across your back, I can see you've had your fun..." The combination of these street-tough, almost-s&m-oriented lyrics and the soul-inflected falsettos that punctuate the chorus makes for a very down-to-earth Hendrix tune that is, yet, filled with metaphor. The traffic signals in this song go from green to red, not to blue, as in "The Wind Cries Mary," a more whispy song. "Traffic" is down-to-Earth, basic rock 'n' roll with an edge.

The song has a lot of the traditional form of Top Forty r&b music, the kind Jimi played as a sideman with the Isley Brothers and King Curtis. It has the constant hook of the chorus, with its "yeahs" and "du du du du" mixed with the refrain, "crosstown traffic," and it has the swagger and misogyny of the r&b attitude ("so hard to get to you...all you do is slow me down, I've got better things on the other side of town"), but in its more total approach to songwriting, you can see the emerging Jimi, telling his story through metaphor—the whole song is metaphor—irony, and the outside drift of his guitar, though there is no real solo break in the song. Jimi just uses his ax in the service of rhythm, as a traditional r&b artist would.

"Traffic" was recorded on a four-track in London on December 20, 1969, but not released as an English single (b/w "Gypsy Eyes") until April, 1969. By this time, it had been overdubbed to 12 or 16 tracks, and that's how it got to *Electric Ladyland*.

Crosstown Traffic

Words and Music by Jimi Hendrix

MANIC DEPRESSION

From the first interchange of single-line bass notes/pause/single-line low-register run/drum shuffle, you know what's coming. "Music sweet music," that's what. This is the simplest of song structures, yet the build is to the combination of arpeggio run and harmonic vocalizing that leads to string-wrenching bends that howl in the night. Yet, contrary to the title, the song is not depressing or even dark, but uplifting due to its sheer beauty.

Yet, Jimi didn't think so! He told *NME* in May of 1967 that "'Manic Depression' is so ugly, you can feel it." Chas Chandler credits himself for the inspiration of the song. In mid-March, 1967 he told an interviewer from *Beat Instrumental*, "I told Jimi one day that he sounded like a manic depressive. It was at a press reception. So while he was answering the questions he came up with a song about manic depressives."

The song is structured on the bass drones that Jimi lays down, with the guitar coming right in and howling away, truly howling. Indeed, when recording this tune, Jimi played the bass himself, using it as punctuation of the recurring riff—not as it's usually done by Noel, a rhythm-oriented backing counterpoint that wants be a lead line, but rather as the basis for the whole riff. The time signature of this tune is 9/8, an unusual, jazzy one for Jimi, propelled by the manic drums of Mitch Mitchell and laden with feedback combined with whammy-bar-shaking vibrato. The feedback is produced, most likely, by placing the guitar neck against the amp's speaker cabinet.

"Manic Depression" was not released as a single, though it was included on the *Are You Experienced?* lp.

Manic Depression

Words and Music by Jimi Hendrix

REMEMBER

Reprise thought this song unremarkable enough to omit from its American release version of *Are You Experienced?* though it did make it to the English one. It was not a single and certainly does not qualify as a "smash hit" by any means. It is a lilting, wistful, loping tune that's not very characteristic of any-period Hendrix, though it was among his earliest repertoire, dating back to that Finsbury Park gig of March 31, 1967, where Jimi torched his first guitar on the "Fire" finale.

The song is about lost love ("Oh, remember, the mockingbird, he used to sing for his supper, babe...but since my baby left me, he ain't sang a tune all day."), like so many pop ditties of the day. The thing that differentiates it is the voice of the poet, talking about birds and bees and meaning lost love that shines through the lyrics and the loping rhythm guitar that refuses to play the same lick twice, even in the same song. In the fade, you can hear Jimi's plaintive, cosmic mumble: "...can you hear me calling you? Come on, baby...hurry home, hurry home."

The song's greatest distinction is that it shows Jimi as a consummate performer, keeping the tune as his guitar spewed chords in counterpoint, even though he really didn't think he had it as a singer. History was to prove him wrong.

N. Carter

Remember

Words and Music by Jimi Hendrix

D7
A
Kiss you for my din– ner babe, now. But a if you don't come back you know I'll
have to starve to death, 'cause I ain't had one kiss all day ______ now.
B♭
Please ______ re – mem– ber,
F7
E♭
you got to re – mem– ber, you got to re –
B♭
F7
mem– ber – our love. Come on back, come on back in my arms. ______
B♭
I'll make ev– 'ry thing that bet – ter.
F7
Outro
Come on baby, hurry up now. Can you hear me
calling you back. Come on baby, stop jiving around
Hurry home, hurry home.

RED HOUSE

© N. Carter

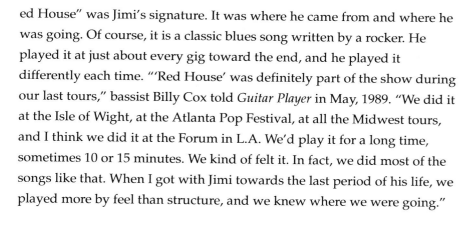

"**R**ed House" was Jimi's signature. It was where he came from and where he was going. Of course, it is a classic blues song written by a rocker. He played it at just about every gig toward the end, and he played it differently each time. "'Red House' was definitely part of the show during our last tours," bassist Billy Cox told *Guitar Player* in May, 1989. "We did it at the Isle of Wight, at the Atlanta Pop Festival, at all the Midwest tours, and I think we did it at the Forum in L.A. We'd play it for a long time, sometimes 10 or 15 minutes. We kind of felt it. In fact, we did most of the songs like that. When I got with Jimi towards the last period of his life, we played more by feel than structure, and we knew where we were going."

It has been said that Jimi wrote it as a tribute to Albert King, another left-handed guitarist whom Jimi looked up to. According to a story in the *St. Louis Post-Dispatch* (April 17, 1986), "Jimi was just out of the army and sat on the steps outside a St. Louis club to listen to Albert King. King liked him and invited him inside and let him play with the band, even though he was not yet a very accomplished musician. King defended Jimi when he sat in with another East St. Louis band and was laughed at by leader Ike Turner for his lack of skill." Indeed, there are some drastic bends of the A-string in "Red House" that come straight out of Albert, and the double-stop bends are killer blues. But Jimi takes the blues *out* with devices such as generating the dominant pitch over the subdominant harmony, while modulating the pitch of the feedback with his right hand. Application of the wah-wah pedal on this nascent blues is another futuristic technique that makes the song a "future classic." Jimi uses the wah-wah about eight different ways, getting tremolo, rhythm, and modulated melody out of it in all kinds of previously unexplored techniques.

There is no bass on the recorded version. Noel told *Guitar Player* in their May, 1989 issue: "Jimi said to us, ' This is a blues in B.' I borrowed a terrible, awful hollow-body electric guitar from someone at the studio...because I like to play along on rhythm....We ended up just recording it. First take, I think. My guitar's bass was turned full up to make a good contrast to Jimi's."

Could Hendrix play the hard blues, John Lee Hooker was asked recently. "Oooh, yeah," the wizened bluesman replied. "He could play anything he wanted. He could play deep blues, what do you think 'Red House' is? That's really hard. That 'Red House' will make you grab your mother and choke her!"

49

Red House

By Jimi Hendrix

Intro

There's a   red house o - ver yon - der.

That's where my   ba – by   stays.

Lord, there's a   red house o - ver yon-der.   Lord, that's where my ba–by   stays.

I ain't been home to see my ba–by   in nine-ty-nine and one–half days.

Wait a   min-ute some-thing's wrong here.

This key won't un–lock this door.   Wait a min-ute some-thing's wrong.

Lord, have mer-cy this key won't un-lock this door. Some-thing's go-ing wrong here.

E7   **D7**

I have a bad, bad feel-in' That my ba—by don't live here no

Gtr. Fill

A7   **E7**   **Gtr. Solo**   **11**

more.   *That's all right, I still have my guitar. Look out now.*

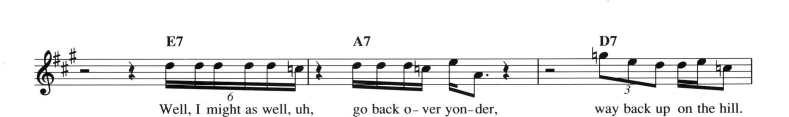

E7   **A7**   **D7**

Well, I might as well, uh, go back o-ver yon-der, way back up on the hill.

Gtr. Fill

A7   **D7**

Lord, I might as well go back o-ver yon-der.

Gtr. Fill

A7   **E7**

Way back yon-der cross the hill. 'Cause if my ba-by don't love me no more,

Outro

D7   **A7**   **A7**   **B♭7**   **A7**

I know her sis—ter will.

FOXEY LADY

This song was inspired, said Jimi later (*Music Maker,* June, 1967), by a lady he lived with for nearly two years—Cathy Etchingham. "I wrote 'Foxey' so long ago," he said. "What we are doing today is as different from that as night from day. Our music is getting uglier. I get my inspiration for songs from everyday things, and girls. Girls can misunderstand you so much—they really can. But it's nice to have them around. One song I wrote is about a girl I used to know. I think she's an acidhead now—and much nicer." He told *NME* some two years later, that the musical inspiration came from Muddy Waters' *Electric Mud* lp: "I swear to God, when I was listening to that album I heard 'Foxey Lady' and 'Purple Haze' in there somewhere."

But "Foxey" has its metal fanatics, too, who swear it is the progenitor of their leather-clad genre. Says K.K. Downing of Judas Priest (*Record Review,* 1980): "I don't think that Hendrix can be put in any school; but I think that "Foxey Lady" is the greatest heavy metal song ever. Go home and play it and turn it up. You'll see what I mean."

"Foxey Lady" was not released as a single, so it is not a smash hit, by any definition, except that it is truly a classic early-Hendrix song that continues to garner airplay today. It first appeared on record in England as part of the bombastic debut *Are You Experienced?* lp. The sonic effects on the guitar are astounding, and were an aural blitzkrieg when it first came out as the album's opening cut. The opening trill, followed by the haunting knell of phased guitar, signalled that this monster player was truly "comin' to gitcha!"

Foxey Lady

Words and Music by Jimi Hendrix

51st ANNIVERSARY

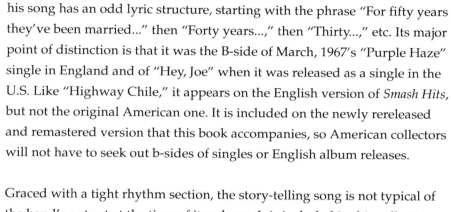

This song has an odd lyric structure, starting with the phrase "For fifty years they've been married..." then "Forty years...," then "Thirty...," etc. Its major point of distinction is that it was the B-side of March, 1967's "Purple Haze" single in England and of "Hey, Joe" when it was released as a single in the U.S. Like "Highway Chile," it appears on the English version of *Smash Hits*, but not the original American one. It is included on the newly rereleased and remastered version that this book accompanies, so American collectors will not have to seek out b-sides of singles or English album releases.

Graced with a tight rhythm section, the story-telling song is not typical of the band's output at the time of its release. It is included in this collection as a historical oddity. And Jimi liked it, as this anecdote illustrates: On May 18, 1967, The Jimi Hendrix Experience received their first fifty-thousand-pound installment from Warner/Reprise Records for the rights to their first album, which had been released in Europe earlier that week. In Frankfurt, Germany, on that day, Jimi, Mitch, and Noel were interviewed by Hans Carl Schmidt for German radio. The deejay asked the group, "Wish yourself a record; which shall we play?" Riding the crest of their third smash single and first album release, Jimi replied with a seemingly obscure request: "How 'bout '51st Anniversary?' "

The song is very ironic and backhanded in tone for Jimi, perhaps because it refers obscurely to Jimi's own personal problems as the product of a "broken home." Jimi's parents had separated when he was a baby, and Jimi got passed around to relatives, then was raised by his father. When he was 15, his mother died. "For twenty years they've been married, they don't get along that good—they're tired of each other, you know how that goes..." the song rambles in its parable of an imaginary couple. "So now you're seventeen, runnin' around havin' your fun." And then the refrain goes, "So you, you say you want to be married... tryin' to put me on a chain, ain't that some shame.. you must be losin' your...sweet little mind!" Then Jimi gets back to his "groove," not wanting to be bothered by thoughts of marriage. Strange song, indeed.

51st Anniversary

By Jimi Hendrix

and talk about.... So you _____ you say you wan – na be mar – ried _____

To Coda ⊕

E

B

I'm gon – na change your mind.

B   A   E   B   A   E   **D. S. al Coda**

⊕ **Coda**

B

Oh, baby,   Trying to put me on a chain.

Ain't that some shame.   You must be losing your,   sshh – hmm,   Sweet little mind.

I ain't ready yet ba – by.   I ain't ready.

E   B

I'm gon – na change _ your   mind. _____

B   A   E

Whew, lode out.   Ow!   I   ain't

B   A   E   B   A

read – y   to get tied down.   I   ain't   read – y,   I   ain't

E   B   A   E

read – y now.   Let me   live   a lit – tle while long – er.   Let me

B   A   E   B   D

live,   let me   live a   lit – tle while long – er.

G   B   D   G   **Outro**

So if you're finished talking, let me get back to my groove.

HIGHWAY CHILE

Recorded in February, 1967, the song was released as the flip side of "The Wind Cries Mary," May 12, 1967. Collectors of English sides will have this one, being on the UK *Smash Hits* as well as the post-1975 English pressings of *War Heroes*. The song is virtually unreleased in the US. Sadly, it was never performed in concert. London's *New Musical Express* described it when it came out on the single as "a finger-clicker in the Chuck Berry style with insistent fuzz guitar. Insidious!"

From the opening twisted and bent chords of the intro and the ballsy refrain, you know this one is from the initial spark of the band in its first full blush of glory. The opening lyric alludes both to the Chuck Berry tune that inspired Jimi most, "Johnny B. Goode," and to his early days slogging the road on the Chitlin' Circuit, backing r&b bands: "His guitar slung across his back, his dusty boots is his Cadillac. Flamin' hair just a-blowin' in the wind, ain't seen a bed so long it's a sin. He left home when he was seventeen, the rest of the world he'd gone to see. And everybody knows, boss, a rolling stone gathers no moss...he's a [*double-bend guitar refrain*] Highway Chile." But it's also Jimi's image of himself as a "rolling stone," a very Greenwich Village image of the vagabond hero. It's not coincidental that this image and "blowin' in the wind" come from Jimi's own vagabond hero, Bob Dylan. The song is a great one, being essentially Jimi's own anthem to the same experiences that inspired Jack Kerouac's *Dharma Bums*, Dylan, and Ramblin' Jack Elliot. It showed Jimi to be much more than just a pop star. He was a folk hero and a deep thinker with a tremendous sense of his own tradition as a troubadour.

Highway Chile

By Jimi Hendrix

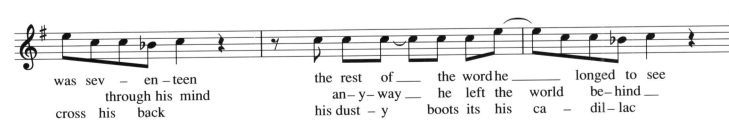